POWER
POSITIVITY

I AM
ENOUGH

Hardie Grant

BOOKS

IF WE STOP DEFINING EACH OTHER BY WHAT WE ARE NOT AND START DEFINING OURSELVES BY WHO WE ARE, WE CAN ALL BE FREER.

Emma Watson

IT MAY NOT BE THE
BEST THERE IS.
ANOTHER WRITER MAY
DO IT MUCH BETTER.
BUT I KNOW WHEN IT'S
THE BEST I CAN DO.

Maya Angelou

I WAS TOLD I WASN'T GOOD ENOUGH,

BUT I JUST CHOSE NOT TO LISTEN.

Khalid

DON'T LET YOURSELF GET IN THE WAY OF THE THINGS THAT PEOPLE LOVE ABOUT YOU.

Machine Gun Kelly

ONE MUST MAKE DO WITH WHAT ONE HAS AND FIGHT WITH SUCH WEAPONS AS ARE WITHIN ONE'S REACH.

Vincent Van Gogh

'ENOUGH' IS A FEAST.

(Buddhist proverb)

I CAN BE
WHOEVER I WANT.
I CAN FEEL
HOWEVER I WANT.

Brie Larson

MANY PEOPLE LIVE HABITUALLY
AS IF THE PRESENT MOMENT
WERE AN OBSTACLE THAT THEY
NEED TO OVERCOME IN ORDER
TO GET TO THE NEXT MOMENT,
AND IMAGINE LIVING YOUR
WHOLE LIFE LIKE THAT. ALWAYS,
THIS MOMENT IS NOT QUITE
GOOD ENOUGH BECAUSE YOU
NEED TO GET TO THE NEXT ONE.

Eckhart Tolle

BEAUTY TO ME IS EMBRACING YOUR IMPERFECTIONS SO THEY BECOME YOUR ASSETS.

Diane Von Furstenberg

YOU WILL NEVER BE
GOOD ENOUGH FOR SOME
PEOPLE, NO MATTER HOW
MUCH YOU TRY. FIND THE
PEOPLE WHO ALREADY
SEE THE GOOD IN YOU.

IT IS NOT HOW MUCH WE HAVE, BUT HOW MUCH WE ENJOY, THAT MAKES HAPPINESS.

CH Spurgeon

EVEN I DON'T WAKE UP LOOKING LIKE CINDY CRAWFORD.

Cindy Crawford

YOUR BODY IS PERFECT THE WAY IT IS.

THE EARTH PROVIDES ENOUGH TO SATISFY EVERY MAN'S NEED BUT NOT EVERY MAN'S GREED.

Mahatma Gandhi

DON'T LET THE NOISE OF OTHERS' OPINIONS DROWN OUT YOUR OWN INNER VOICE. AND MOST IMPORTANT, HAVE THE COURAGE TO FOLLOW YOUR HEART AND INTUITION.

Steve Jobs

YOU ALREADY HAVE ACHIEVEMENTS TO BE PROUD OF. NOW YOU CAN BUILD ON THEM.

THINK OF THE PEOPLE YOU LOVE. DO YOU LOVE THEM BECAUSE THEY ARE PERFECT, OR JUST BECAUSE?

IF YOU WANT TO BE RESPECTED
BY OTHERS THE GREAT THING
IS TO RESPECT YOURSELF.
ONLY BY THAT, ONLY BY SELF-
RESPECT WILL YOU COMPEL
OTHERS TO RESPECT YOU.

Fyodor Dostoevsky

WHY SHOULD I STRIVE FOR PERFECTION, IF I AM ALREADY GOOD ENOUGH?

Leo Tolstoy

THERE IS NO SCARCITY OF LOVE. YOU DESERVE IT.

DON'T LET YOURSELF BE DEFINED BY YOUR WORST DAY.

ACCEPTING WHAT YOU CAN'T CHANGE STARTS WITH ACCEPTING YOURSELF.

**WHEN YOUR OWN
CUP IS FULL,
YOU CAN HELP
FILL UP OTHERS.**

**YOUR TIME IS LIMITED,
SO DON'T WASTE IT LIVING
SOMEONE ELSE'S LIFE.**

Steve Jobs

THERE IS MORE THAN ONE WAY TO BE GREAT. YOU WILL FIND THE RIGHT ONE FOR YOU.

YOU ARE
COMPLETE,
ALL ON
YOUR OWN.

WHOEVER IS DISSATISFIED WITH HIMSELF IS CONTINUALLY READY FOR REVENGE, AND WE OTHERS WILL BE HIS VICTIMS.

Friedrich Nietzsche

DON'T LOOK DOWN ON PEOPLE, AND DON'T PUT PEOPLE ON PEDESTALS. SEE PEOPLE FOR WHO THEY ARE: EQUAL TO YOU BUT DIFFERENT.

Mark Ruffalo

**YOU ARE
ALLOWED TO
STOP TRYING
TO CHANGE
YOURSELF.**

I IDENTIFY
AS WHAT I AM.

Andreja Pejic

YOU MAY NOT CONTROL ALL THE EVENTS THAT HAPPEN TO YOU BUT YOU CAN DECIDE NOT TO BE REDUCED BY THEM.

Maya Angelou

PERFECT IS THE ENEMY OF GOOD.

**OUR BODIES
ARE OUR
GARDENS.**

William Shakespeare

I'M ME, AND I'M LIKE NOBODY ELSE.

Lena Horne

**ONE SHOULD LOOK LONG
AND CAREFULLY AT ONESELF
BEFORE ONE CONSIDERS
JUDGING OTHERS.**

Moliere

TO LIVE AT ALL IS MIRACLE ENOUGH.

Mervyn Peake

HAPPINESS RESIDES NOT IN POSSESSIONS AND NOT IN GOLD, THE FEELING OF HAPPINESS DWELLS IN THE SOUL.

Democritus

NO BIRD SOARS TOO HIGH, IF HE SOARS WITH HIS OWN WINGS.

William Blake

WE CAN'T ALL DO EVERYTHING.

Virgil

GRATITUDE TURNS WHAT YOU HAVE INTO ENOUGH.

I CANNOT AND
WILL NOT CUT MY
CONSCIENCE TO
SUIT THIS YEAR'S
FASHIONS.

Lillian Helman

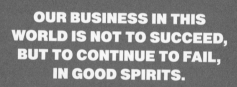

OUR BUSINESS IN THIS WORLD IS NOT TO SUCCEED, BUT TO CONTINUE TO FAIL, IN GOOD SPIRITS.

Robert Louis Stevenson

YOU DO NOT NEED TO BECOME GOOD ENOUGH, YOU ALREADY ARE GOOD ENOUGH.

IF YOU'VE EVER BEEN CALLED
DUMB, UNATTRACTIVE,
OVERWEIGHT, UNWORTHY,
UNTALENTED – WELL SO
HAVE I. WHATEVER YOU DO
DON'T LET NEGATIVITY OF
PEOPLE PROJECTING THEIR
OWN SELF-DOUBTS ON YOU
DETER YOU FROM YOUR FOCUS.

Beyoncé

YOUR NEED FOR ACCEPTANCE
CAN MAKE YOU INVISIBLE IN
THIS WORLD ... YOU WILL ONLY
EVER HAVE TWO CHOICES:
LOVE OR FEAR. CHOOSE LOVE
AND DON'T EVER LET FEAR
TURN YOU AGAINST YOUR
PLAYFUL HEART.

Jim Carrey

WHAT WE CALL FATE DOES NOT COME INTO US FROM THE OUTSIDE BUT EMERGES FROM US.

Rainer Maria Rilke

**WHAT IS A WEED?
A PLANT WHOSE
VIRTUES HAVE NOT YET
BEEN DISCOVERED.**

Ralph Waldo Emerson

WHEN YOU FEEL THE WORST ABOUT YOURSELF,

TREAT YOURSELF THE MOST KINDLY.

THERE'S ONLY ONE WAY OF BEING COMFORTABLE, AND THAT IS TO STOP RUNNING AROUND AFTER HAPPINESS.

Edith Wharton

IN THE DEPTHS OF WINTER, I FINALLY LEARNED THAT WITHIN ME THERE LAY AN INVINCIBLE SUMMER.

Albert Camus

JUST TRUST YOURSELF AND YOU'LL LEARN THE ART OF LIVING.

Goethe

**TAKE REST;
A FIELD THAT HAS
RESTED GIVES
A BOUNTIFUL CROP.**

Ovid

I HAVE FOUND THAT I GET
BRAVER AND I'M LESS
JUDGEMENTAL OF MYSELF
NOW THAT I'M OLDER. I HAVE
WRINKLES AND I'M THINKING
'SO WHAT? I DON'T CARE'.

Jane Fonda

LIVE ALL YOU CAN; IT'S A
MISTAKE NOT TO. IT DOESN'T
SO MUCH MATTER WHAT YOU
DO IN PARTICULAR, SO LONG
AS YOU HAVE YOUR LIFE.
IF YOU HAVEN'T HAD THAT,
WHAT *HAVE* YOU HAD?

Henry James

EVERYONE MAKES MISTAKES. FORGIVE YOURSELF.

**THE MOST COMMON
FORM OF DESPAIR IS
NOT BEING WHO YOU ARE.**

Soren Kierkegaard

A WISE MAN DOES NOT GRIEVE FOR THE THINGS HE DOESN'T HAVE BUT REJOICES IN THOSE HE DOES HAVE.

Epicetetus

I AM THE MASTER
OF MY FATE;
I AM THE CAPTAIN
OF MY SOUL.

WE Henley

IF YOU HAVE NO CONFIDENCE IN SELF YOU ARE TWICE DEFEATED IN THE RACE OF LIFE. WITH CONFIDENCE YOU HAVE WON EVEN BEFORE YOU HAVE STARTED.

Marcus Garvey

WE HAVE TO JUST
BLOCK OUT ALL THAT
NOISE AND BE LIKE
'NO I AM ENOUGH AND
I'M GOOD ENOUGH
AND I AM PRETTY
ENOUGH AND I'M
SMART ENOUGH.'

Alisha Boe

LONELINESS IS THE POVERTY OF SELF; SOLITUDE IS THE RICHNESS OF SELF.

May Sarton

**DO WHAT YOU LOVE
AND LOVE WHAT YOU DO
AND EVERYTHING
ELSE IS DETAIL.**

Martina Navratilova

**WHEREVER YOU GO,
GO WITH ALL YOUR HEART.**

Confucius

NO ONE WAS BORN SUCCESSFUL. WE ARE ALL SOMEWHERE ON THE JOURNEY TO OUR BEST SELVES.

YOU SPEND A LOT OF TIME
JUST TRYING TO BE LIKED
AND YOU GET REALLY WORRIED
ABOUT DO PEOPLE LIKE WHAT
I DID OR DO PEOPLE APPRECIATE
MY WORK AND I THINK THAT
HAVING THE GUTS TO JUST
BE YOURSELF SOMETIMES IS
HARDER THAN PEOPLE THINK.

Ashton Kutcher

THERE'S A REASON WHY
YOU THINK THE WAY YOU DO
AND WANT TO DO THE THINGS
YOU DO AND YOU JUST CAN'T
LET ANYBODY TELL YOU
'DON'T DO IT'. ESPECIALLY
YOU – DON'T ALLOW *YOU*
TO TELL YOU NOT TO DO IT.

Bradley Cooper

YOU CAN'T TRULY ACCEPT OTHER PEOPLE UNTIL YOU ACCEPT YOURSELF.

Emma Watson

I ALWAYS SAY THERE'S
NO SUCH THING
AS SECOND CHANCES
– YOU GET AS MANY
CHANCES AS YOU
WANT IN THIS WORLD.

Aaron Eckhart

**YOUR VALUE
IS NOT MEASURED
BY WHAT YOU
LOOK LIKE.**

THERE'S ONLY SO MUCH
YOU CAN PRETEND.
AT THE END OF THE DAY,
IT'S THE CORE OF YOU
THAT MATTERS.

Annabelle Wallis

IT'S IMPORTANT TO LISTEN
TO EVERYONE, AS MANY PEOPLE
AS YOU CAN AND GET THEIR INPUT
BUT THEN FINALLY YOU HAVE
TO MAKE YOUR OWN DECISION
ABOUT WHAT YOU'RE GONNA
DO. AND THAT'S IT, THAT'S
WHAT YOU FEEL AND THAT'S
THE MOST IMPORTANT THING.

Robert de Niro

WE SHOULD NEVER, EVER
COMPARE OURSELVES TO
OTHERS ... I JUST TRY TO
HONESTLY TRY AND WORK
ON WHAT I HAVE.

Jennifer Lopez

I'M THE ONE THAT'S CONTROLLING MY JOY AND HAPPINESS.

Derek Luke

**I HAVE NO REGRETS.
I HAVE ZERO.
I'M EXACTLY WHERE
I WANT TO BE.**

Julie Delpy

YOU CAN'T CONTROL HOW OTHERS SEE YOU, BUT YOU CAN CONTROL HOW YOU THINK ABOUT YOURSELF.

WE ALL HAVE STRENGTHS AND WEAKNESSES. THESE ARE WHAT MAKE YOU, YOU.

TRY LOOKING AT YOURSELF IN THE BEST LIGHT. THEN BUILD ON WHAT YOU LOVE ABOUT YOURSELF.

**KNOWING YOU ARE
ENOUGH WILL
FREE YOU TO TRY
NEW THINGS.**

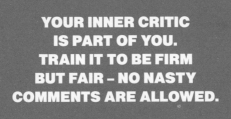

YOUR INNER CRITIC
IS PART OF YOU.
TRAIN IT TO BE FIRM
BUT FAIR – NO NASTY
COMMENTS ARE ALLOWED.

PRACTISE GRATITUDE FOR THE WONDERFUL THINGS YOU HAVE AND THE WONDERFUL THINGS YOU ARE.

YOU ARE WORTHY OF BEING LOVED.

THE STORY YOU TELL YOURSELF IS POWERFUL. SAY IT OUT LOUD: I AM GOOD ENOUGH.

GETTING COMPLIMENTS FROM OTHERS WILL BOOST YOU FOR A SHORT WHILE, BUT LOVING YOURSELF WILL BE WITH YOU EVERY DAY FOR YOUR WHOLE LIFE.

IT'S NORMAL TO
CARE WHAT OTHERS
THINK ABOUT YOU,
BUT WHAT YOU
THINK ABOUT
YOURSELF IS THE
MOST IMPORTANT
OPINION OF ALL.

DON'T MAKE YOURSELF SMALLER TO SUIT OTHER PEOPLE.

YOU DON'T NEED TO HAVE PERFECT SELF-CONFIDENCE TO FEEL GOOD ENOUGH. YOU ALREADY DESERVE IT.

YOU'RE ALWAYS GOING TO HAVE AN EBB AND FLOW. IT'S GONNA BE TOUGH SOME DAYS AND IT'S GONNA BE GREAT OTHERS.

Michelle Monaghan

**THIS ABOVE ALL:
TO THINE OWN
SELF BE TRUE.**

William Shakespeare

**YOU CAN'T ALWAYS
BE TALL ENOUGH, QUICK
ENOUGH OR CLEVER ENOUGH,
BUT WHAT IF YOU WERE
GENTLE ENOUGH, BRAVE
ENOUGH OR KIND ENOUGH?**

THE PERFECT PERSON YOU
ADMIRE HAS ALL THEIR OWN
DOUBTS, HEALTH PROBLEMS,
BAD DAYS AND EMBARRASSING
STORIES. THEY ARE GREAT,
BUT SO ARE YOU.

Published in 2022 by
Hardie Grant Books, an imprint
of Hardie Grant Publishing

Hardie Grant Books (London)
5th & 6th Floors
52–54 Southwark Street
London SE1 1UN

Hardie Grant Books (Melbourne)
Building 1, 658 Church Street
Richmond, Victoria 3121

hardiegrantbooks.com

British Library Cataloguing-in-
Publication Data. A catalogue
record for this book is available
from the British Library.

I AM ENOUGH
by Hardie Grant Books

ISBN: 9781784885656

Publishing Director: Kajal Mistry
Acting Publishing Director:
Emma Hopkin
Commissioning Editor: Kate Burkett
Text curated by: Satu Fox
Editorial Assistant: Harriet Thornley
Design: Claire Warner Studio

Colour Reproduction by p2d
Printed and bound in China by
Leo Paper Products Ltd.